THE BENEFITS OF REMOTE WORKING

Unlock the Freedom and Success of Working from Anywhere

Ray Goodwin

CONTENTS

Title Page

Copyright

Liability Disclaimer

Chapter 1: Introduction   1

Chapter 2: Remote Work and Productivity   4

Chapter 3: Remote Work and Work-Life Balance   8

Chapter 4: Remote Work and Cost Savings   12

Chapter 5: Remote Work and Employee Satisfaction   17

Chapter 6: Remote Work and Collaboration   21

Chapter 7: Remote Work and Recruitment   29

Chapter 8: Remote Work and Cybersecurity   34

Chapter 9: Remote Work and Legal Considerations   37

Chapter 10: Remote Work and Leadership   40

Chapter 11: Remote Work and Project Management   44

Chapter 12: Remote Work and Performance Management   47

Chapter 13: Remote Work and Diversity, Equity, and   50
Inclusion (DEI)

Chapter 14: Remote Work and Entrepreneurship   54

Chapter 15: Remote Work and Education   57

Chapter 16: Remote Work and Mental Health   62

Chapter 17: Remote Work and Social Responsibility 66

Chapter 18: Remote Work and Future Trends 70

Chapter 19: Remote Work and Personal Development 74

Chapter 20: Conclusion 78

About The Author 81

LIABILITY DISCLAIMER

The information contained within this book is intended for informational purposes only and should not be construed as legal or professional advice. The authors and publishers of this book are not responsible for any losses or damages that may arise from the use of the information contained within.

The reader assumes full responsibility for any decisions made based on the information in this book. The authors and publishers do not endorse any particular method, service or product mentioned in this book and are not responsible for any consequences resulting from their use.

The reader should exercise caution and discretion when making life changing decisions, and should be aware of the risks and potential consequences of their actions. This book is not a substitute for professional or legal advice and should not be relied upon as such.

By reading and using the information in this book, the reader acknowledges and agrees to hold harmless the authors, publishers, and any other parties involved in the creation or distribution of this book from any and all liability, claims, damages, or losses that may arise from their use of the information contained herein.

CHAPTER 1:
INTRODUCTION

Welcome to "The Benefits of Remote Working," a practical guide to the world of remote work. In the current digital age, the traditional office model is rapidly evolving, and more and more businesses are shifting towards remote work. Encouraging employees to work from home is becoming increasingly popular as it offers a wide range of benefits for both companies and individuals.

As an author who has spent over 25 years working online, I have had the opportunity to experience firsthand the advantages that remote working can bring. This book is designed for anyone who wants to learn about the changes currently taking place in the workplace and how they can embrace these changes.

Throughout this book, I will delve into the various ways in which remote working can improve productivity, reduce stress levels, and increase job satisfaction. I will also explore how companies can benefit from adopting flexible working arrangements by improving their bottom line through lower overheads and increased employee retention rates.

Whether you're an entrepreneur looking to establish a remote team or simply considering making the switch yourself, "The Benefits of Remote Working" provides valuable insights that will help you navigate this exciting new world of work.

In recent years, remote work has become increasingly popular as a result of advances in technology and changes in work culture. With the outbreak of the COVID-19 pandemic, remote work has become the new normal for millions of workers worldwide. This shift has demonstrated the importance of remote work and its potential for transforming the way we work in the future.

Remote work, also referred to as telecommuting or teleworking, can be defined as work that is done outside of the traditional office setting and typically involves the use of technology to connect workers with their colleagues, clients, and customers. This includes working from home, coworking spaces, and other remote locations.

Remote work has a long history dating back to the 1970s when technology began to emerge as a viable alternative to traditional office work. The concept of remote work gained traction in the 1990s with the advent of the internet and various communication technologies such as email, video conferencing, and instant messaging. In recent years, remote work has become more commonplace, with many companies adopting remote work policies to attract and retain talent, reduce overhead costs, and improve work-life balance for their employees.

In the modern business world, remote work has become increasingly important due to the need for flexibility and agility in a rapidly changing market. Remote work offers numerous benefits for both employers and employees, including increased productivity, reduced costs, improved work-life balance, and greater employee satisfaction.

However, remote work also presents unique challenges, including distractions, the lack of face-to-face interaction, and managing a remote team. The purpose of this book is to explore the benefits of remote work while providing strategies for overcoming the challenges that come with it.

In the following chapters, we will delve deeper into the various aspects of remote work, including its impact on productivity, work-life balance, cost savings, employee satisfaction, collaboration, leadership, performance management, diversity, and inclusion, entrepreneurship, education, mental health, and social responsibility. We will also examine future trends in remote work and provide recommendations for embracing remote work opportunities.

As we navigate this unprecedented time of remote work, it is important to recognize the potential for remote work to transform the way we work and live. By embracing the benefits of remote work and overcoming its challenges, we can create a more productive, flexible, and fulfilling work environment for ourselves and future generations.

CHAPTER 2: REMOTE WORK AND PRODUCTIVITY

Remote work has steadily increased over the last decade, and since the pandemic, it has become the new norm for many businesses worldwide. The major concern businesses had when it came to remote working was a decrease in productivity. However, numerous studies have shown that remote working does not hinder the productivity of remote employees. In fact, some studies indicate that remote employees are more productive than their traditional office counterparts.

Impact of Remote Working on Productivity

Remote working provides employees with the freedom to set up their workspace, reducing the distractions they would typically face in a traditional office setting. Employees can customize their work environment to facilitate productivity and cultivate routine that works best for them. This level of flexibility results in fewer interruptions and more opportunities for focused work. Additionally, remote employees can construct a conducive work environment tailored to their individual needs.

Distractions and How to Avoid Them

Working from home blurs the boundaries between work and

personal life, which can eventually lead to distractions. To maintain a high level of productivity, remote employees require a high degree of focus. Setting up a dedicated workspace that is clean and free from clutter is essential. A dedicated workspace makes it easier for the employee to start concentrating from the moment they begin working.

Time Management Strategies for Remote Workers

Successful remote workers prioritize their tasks to ensure they complete the most important and time-sensitive work first. An online task manager like Trello is essential when it comes to creating a comprehensive to-do list for the workday. It is also essential to set boundaries to maintain productivity, deciding on a regular work schedule and sticking to it. Creating a daily routine helps in maintaining consistency, which is necessary for productivity and work-life balance.

Best Practices in Remote Team Collaboration

Communication is vital in any organization, but it is particularly crucial for remote teams who don't have the luxury of physical proximity. Remote workers need to have access to reliable collaboration tools. Examples of collaboration tools are Slack and Zoom. These tools offer an environment optimized for virtual communication with features such as video and audio conferencing, instant messaging, screen sharing, and file-sharing capabilities.

Tools and Technologies for Remote Work Productivity

There are several online tools that remote workers can use to enhance productivity. Video conferencing tools like Zoom, Skype, or Google Meet offer virtual collaboration tools, allowing remote workers to connect seamlessly from anywhere in the world. Cloud storage services like Dropbox, Google Drive, and OneDrive provide a remote team with reliable and secure access to company files and documents.

Building a Productive Remote Work Environment

Productivity is directly related to the work environment. When employees work in an environment conducive to their most productive work style, they are more likely to remain focused, motivated and produce higher-quality work. Employers should encourage flexibility and autonomy so that employees can personalize their workspaces, creating a workspace that reflects their personality and style.

Common Productivity Myths About Remote Working

There are numerous misconceptions about remote working. One of the most common myths is that remote employees are slackers who don't work hard. The truth is that remote employees actually tend to work longer hours than traditional office employees because they end up working at almost any time of the day.

Measuring Productivity in Remote Work Settings

Measuring productivity in a remote work environment is essential, but it is not an easy task. Employers can measure productivity through relevant metrics, which can include the number of completed projects, average workload per employee, the quality of their work, adhering to timelines, and the time it takes for employees to complete an assigned task. By keeping track of team progress, employers can identify areas in which they need to improve and celebrate employee success.

Remote work continues to transform the way businesses operate, and, as a result, it's essential to maintain high productivity levels. Businesses must equip their remote workers with the necessary tools and resources to help them optimize their work style.

Remote work comes with its own set of perks and challenges, and when managed effectively, it can lead to increased productivity levels, happier employees, and business growth.

CHAPTER 3: REMOTE WORK AND WORK-LIFE BALANCE

Remote work has many benefits such as improved productivity, reduced costs, and increased employee satisfaction. One of the most significant advantages is work-life balance. In traditional office settings, the line between work and personal life is often blurred. Employees can become consumed by work demands which can negatively impact their personal life. Remote work offers the flexibility to balance work and personal life, improving employees' overall well-being.

Setting boundaries

Setting boundaries between work and personal life is essential in remote work environments. Without set boundaries, remote workers can quickly become consumed by work and may neglect their personal life. It is essential to set guidelines that establish personal time and work time. Maintain a daily schedule that includes time for personal activities such as exercise, leisure, and socializing. Additionally, establishing a designated workspace can be beneficial in separating your work life from your personal life. Having a designated workspace can help remote workers switch from work to personal life mentally.

Flexible work schedules

Flexible work schedules are another benefit of remote working, allowing workers to complete work tasks when it's convenient for them. Remote workers don't have to wake up early to commute to work or get home late. They have the flexibility to schedule their work around their personal life. This increases the quality of their personal life while also allowing for increased productivity in their work life.

Social Connections

Social connections and avoiding isolation is important in maintaining work-life balance in remote work environments. Remote workers can feel lonely as they lack face-to-face interaction with coworkers. This can lead to feelings of isolation. To maintain social connections and avoid isolation, remote workers should work to connect with their colleagues virtually. Using instant messaging or video chat applications can help recreate the same level of interaction experienced in a traditional office setting. Remote workers can also engage in social activities such as virtual team building activities.

Stress management

Stress management is important in remote work environments, and it's crucial to find ways to manage stress to maintain work-life balance. Remote workers should engage in physical activities such as yoga or exercise to relieve stress. Additionally, practicing mindfulness and taking breaks from work activities can help reduce stress levels. Remote workers should set aside time for activities they enjoy such as reading or listening to music to reduce stress levels.

Healthy Habits

Encouraging physical activity and healthy habits is essential in maintaining work-life balance in remote work settings. Long periods of sitting in front of a screen can negatively impact overall health. Remote workers should take short breaks frequently to stretch, walk or engage in physical exercises. Additionally, remote workers should take conscious steps to maintain healthy eating habits. Establishing proper eating habits can help increase energy levels, improving work productivity.

Overcoming challenges

Overcoming challenges of balancing work and personal life is critical in remote work settings. Remote workers will often face challenges in balancing work and life responsibilities. This is common in work environments, but remote workers can mitigate these challenges. Remote workers should communicate their challenges with their managers, developing strategies to overcome them. Technology solutions can also help to overcome some challenges. For example, project management tools can help remote workers collaborate effectively with colleagues in different time zones. Additionally, remote workers can use time-tracking tools to manage their workflow properly.

Best practices

Best practices for maintaining work-life balance in remote work settings should be implemented to maximize the benefits of remote work. Establishing a daily routine can help maintain the perfect balance between work and personal life. Remote workers should schedule time specifically for personal activities and relaxation. This ensures that they have enough downtime to recharge, improving their overall well-being. Additionally, setting boundaries and sticking to them helps remote workers identify the start and end of their workday.

Remote workers can benefit from maintaining work-life balance. It provides them with the flexibility to balance work and personal life, improving their well-being. It's important to establish guidelines that ensure a balance between work and personal life, making remote work an attractive option for employees.

CHAPTER 4: REMOTE WORK AND COST SAVINGS

As businesses seek to maximize their profits, one aspect that is often scrutinized is the cost of running their operations. In traditional office settings, businesses have to incur several expenses, including rent, utilities, and office supplies. These expenses can add up quickly, especially for businesses that operate in large facilities or major cities. However, with the advent of remote work, businesses can save considerably on their operating expenses. In this chapter, we'll explore the cost-saving benefits of remote working and how businesses can maximize these savings.

Reduction in Office Space and Overhead Costs

One of the most significant cost-saving benefits of remote work is the reduction in office space and overhead costs. When employees work remotely, businesses do not have to provide office space, furniture, equipment, and other supplies. This can save businesses a considerable amount of money, especially those operating in large cities where rent can be exorbitant.

Additionally, remote work eliminates the need for businesses to invest in large facilities that can accommodate all their employees. Businesses can rent smaller office spaces or even operate completely virtual offices, which can save them thousands of dollars annually.

For instance, several large companies such as Twitter, Shopify, and Square announced plans to adopt a "remote-first" approach, which means that employees can work remotely indefinitely. Shopify, a leading e-commerce platform, announced that it will keep its offices closed until 2021 and allow all employees to work remotely permanently. The company will also cover the costs of equipment and home office expenses for its employees.

Savings in Transportation and Travel Expenses

Remote work also eliminates the need for employees to commute daily to their workplaces. Commuting can be time-consuming and expensive, especially for employees who live far from their offices. It can also be a significant source of stress for employees who have to worry about traffic, parking, and other inconveniences.

With remote work, employees can save on commuting costs and reduce their carbon footprint. According to a report by Global Workplace Analytics, remote work can save employees up to $7,000 annually in transportation costs. Furthermore, businesses can also reduce their travel expenses by adopting remote work. Traveling for business meetings, conferences, or training can be a significant expense for businesses, but remote work can eliminate these expenses completely.

The Impact of Remote Work on Employee Salaries and Benefits

Another cost-saving benefit that businesses can realize from remote work is the impact on employee salaries and benefits. When businesses hire remote workers, they can offer lower salaries than they would for employees who work in-house. This is because remote workers do not require the same geographic compensation as in-house employees.

Additionally, businesses do not have to provide benefits such as health insurance, retirement plans, and other perks when employees work remotely. In some cases, remote workers may be responsible for their own benefits, which can save businesses a considerable amount of money. For example, a business that hires a remote worker in a country with universal healthcare may not be required to provide health insurance benefits.

Tax Benefits of Remote Working

Businesses can also realize several tax benefits from adopting remote work. For instance, when businesses provide employees with home office equipment such as laptops, printers, or phones, they can claim tax deductions for these expenses. In some cases, businesses can also claim tax deductions for the costs of utilities and rent for employees' home offices.

Additionally, businesses can save money on taxes by hiring remote workers in other states or countries where taxes are lower. In the United States, businesses are subject to different tax rates in each state, and hiring remote workers in states with lower taxes can be an effective way to lower their tax burden.

Strategies for Maximizing Cost Savings in Remote Work Setups

To maximize the cost-saving benefits of remote work, businesses can adopt several strategies. First, businesses can analyze their operating expenses and identify which costs can be eliminated or reduced with remote work.

Secondly, businesses can promote energy efficiency in their remote work setups by encouraging employees to use energy-efficient devices and reduce their carbon footprint. This can save businesses money on utility bills and promote environmental sustainability.

Thirdly, businesses can provide employees with the necessary equipment and tools to work remotely effectively. For instance, businesses can provide employees with dedicated home offices, ergonomic chairs and desks to promote employee comfort and productivity.

Lastly, businesses can adopt a results-based approach to remote work. This means that instead of focusing on the hours that employees work, businesses should measure employees' results and productivity. This can promote a culture of trust and accountability and ensure that businesses maximize the productivity of their remote workforce.

Calculating Cost Savings from Remote Working Arrangements

To evaluate the cost-saving benefits of remote work, businesses need to keep track of their expenses and calculate their cost savings regularly. They can use software tools or spreadsheets to track their expenses and identify areas for improvement.

For instance, businesses can compare their expenses before and after adopting remote work and calculate the percentage of cost savings. Businesses can also track the impact of remote work on their bottom line by monitoring their revenue and profits.

The Impact of Remote Work on Economic Growth and Sustainability

Remote work not only benefits businesses, but it also has a significant impact on economic growth and sustainability. Remote work can help reduce traffic congestion, air pollution, and carbon footprint, which can promote environmental sustainability. Additionally, remote work can help distribute economic opportunities to different geographical locations, reduce income inequality, and promote economic growth.

According to a report by Upwork, remote work can add up to $2.2 trillion to the global economy annually. Furthermore, remote work can open up job opportunities for workers who live in rural areas or developing countries. This can promote economic growth and improve the quality of life for workers who have limited job opportunities.

Conclusion

Remote work offers significant cost-saving benefits for businesses that adopt this model. By eliminating or reducing office space, transportation, and travel expenses, remote work can save businesses money while promoting economic growth and sustainability. Businesses can maximize these savings by adopting energy-efficient practices, providing remote workers with the necessary equipment and tools, and measuring employee results instead of the hours worked. Overall, remote work represents a cost-effective and sustainable solution for businesses looking to succeed in the modern world.

CHAPTER 5: REMOTE WORK AND EMPLOYEE SATISFACTION

Remote work has become an increasingly popular option for both employees and employers. As companies embrace remote work, they are discovering that it benefits their employees in many ways. However, there are also challenges to remote work that can impact employee satisfaction. In this chapter, we will examine the impact that remote work has on employee satisfaction and discuss best practices for ensuring employee satisfaction in remote work settings.

Increased Job Satisfaction and Motivation

Remote work can lead to higher levels of job satisfaction and motivation for many employees. When employees have the flexibility to work where and when they want, they often experience a greater sense of autonomy and control over their work. This can be empowering and motivating, leading to increased levels of engagement and satisfaction.

Improving Work-Life Integration and Work Flexibility

One of the biggest benefits of remote work is the ability to achieve a better work-life balance. For employees with children or other family obligations, remote work can be a lifeline, allowing them to work from home and care for their loved ones at the same time. This can help to reduce stress and improve mental health, which can have a positive impact on employee satisfaction.

Diversity and Inclusivity in Remote Work Environments

Remote work can also promote diversity and inclusivity in the workplace. When employees have the ability to work from anywhere, companies can hire talent from all over the world. This can lead to more diverse teams and can help to break down barriers to employment based on location or mobility issues.

Psychological Benefits of Remote Working

Remote workers may also experience psychological benefits that lead to increased satisfaction. For some workers, the office environment can be a source of stress and anxiety. Remote work can provide a quieter, more personalized work environment that can be more conducive to productivity and comfort. Additionally, remote work can reduce commuting time, which can lead to less stress and a better overall quality of life.

Increasing Employee Engagement and Retention

Remote work can also lead to increased employee engagement and retention. When employees feel empowered and have greater control over their work, they are more likely to stay at a company for longer periods of time. Additionally, remote work can provide a more flexible work environment that can be more appealing to employees with diverse needs.

Overcoming Challenges of Remote Work on Employee Satisfaction

While remote work has many benefits, there are still challenges that can impact employee satisfaction. One challenge is the lack of face-to-face interaction between remote workers and their colleagues. This can lead to feelings of isolation and loneliness, which can negatively impact mental health and job satisfaction. To overcome this challenge, companies can make an effort to connect remote workers through virtual meetings, messaging apps, and other forms of communication technology.

Another challenge is the potential for burnout. Remote workers may feel a constant pressure to be available and productive, which can lead to burnout and a decreased sense of satisfaction with their work. To prevent burnout, companies should encourage their remote workers to take breaks, set limits on their work hours, and find other ways to recharge and renew their energy levels.

Best Practices for Ensuring Employee Satisfaction in Remote Work Settings

To ensure employee satisfaction in remote work settings, companies should focus on creating a supportive work culture that values employee happiness and well-being. This can include providing regular feedback and recognition, offering training and development opportunities, and providing resources for mental health and well-being. Additionally, companies should ensure that remote workers have the tools and technologies they need to do their job effectively, such as access to reliable internet connections and collaborative tools that help to facilitate communication and teamwork.

Conclusion

Remote work can have a significant impact on employee satisfaction, motivation, and engagement. By creating a supportive work environment, companies can help their remote workers to thrive and grow in their roles. As companies continue to embrace remote work, it is important that they also make an effort to address the challenges that can impact employee satisfaction. With the right strategies and tools in place, remote work can be a rewarding and fulfilling option for both employees and employers.

CHAPTER 6:
REMOTE WORK AND COLLABORATION

Collaboration is an essential aspect of work, and remote working should not be a hindrance. Remote workers must work collaboratively to achieve team goals and outcomes just like in an office setting. However, remote collaboration poses unique challenges that teams must address to foster effective communication, teamwork and a positive work culture that will enable the team to succeed.

Importance of Collaboration in Remote Work Environments

Collaboration helps remote workers to feel like they are part of a team. It involves sharing information, ideas and working together to achieve common objectives. Remote collaboration provides flexibility that is necessary to ensure that the team stays cohesive despite being physically apart. Collaboration ensures that remote teams have proper communication channels to stay informed and updated on key issues.

Types of Remote Collaboration

Remote workers have numerous options for collaboration that they can embrace to ensure effective team communication. These include:

1. Video Conferencing

Video conferencing is one of the essential tools of remote collaboration. It provides a platform for remote team members to have face-to-face conversations that are vital in building trust and staying updated on the team's progress. It also allows team members to engage in non-verbal communication such as facial expressions.

2. Instant messaging

Instant messaging provides a platform for impromptu or informal conversations, just as in an office setting. It is vital for remote team members to have access to this communication channel as it allows quick interactions and makes the communication process seamless.

3. Email

Emails play a critical role in the remote working environment. They are useful in conveying information, sharing documents and updates, and maintaining archival records of previous conversations.

4. Project management tools

Project management tools such as Trello, Asana, Jira, and others are essential in ensuring that remote teams manage their projects effectively. They enable team members to assign tasks, set deadlines, track progress, and monitor dependencies.

Strategies for Effective Remote Communication

Remote communication should be clear, concise, and timely. Below are some strategies for ensuring effective remote communication:

1. Clear and timely communication

Communication should be clear, concise, and accurate to avoid misunderstandings. It should also be timely to ensure that team members stay up-to-date with project progress and that team members' concerns and issues are addressed at the earliest.

2. Use video conferencing for critical meetings

Video calls are essential in ensuring that the team stays connected and informed. Teams should use video conferencing to conduct critical meetings such as project kick-offs, status meetings, and project retrospectives.

3. Consider different time zones

Team members could be in different time zones, meaning that they start and finish work at different times. It is essential to consider this when scheduling meetings and deadlines to ensure that everyone has an equal opportunity to participate.

4. Provide a clear agenda

Providing a clear meeting agenda in advance will help attendees to prepare appropriately for the meeting, facilitating effective discussions and decision-making processes.

Managing Conflicts in Remote Work Teams

Conflict management is essential for any team to thrive, and remote teams are no exception. Conflicts are inevitable in any working environment but can quickly escalate if not addressed. Below are some strategies for managing conflicts within remote teams:

1. Encourage open communication

Encouraging open communication enables team members to express their concerns freely and openly. This helps to prevent situations from escalating and helps to resolve conflicts quickly.

2. Address conflicts immediately

It is important to address conflicts as soon as they arise, rather than letting them fester. Addressing conflicts quickly helps to prevent situations from worsening and ensures that the team operates smoothly.

3. Build a positive work culture

Building a positive work culture is essential to fostering a supportive environment where conflicts are managed effectively. Remote teams can build a culture of respect, trust, and collaboration by establishing clear communication channels, upholding team values, and conducting team-building activities.

Tools and Technologies for Remote Collaboration

Remote teams need tools and technologies that facilitate effective communication, collaboration, and project management to succeed. Below are some tools that remote teams can use for collaboration:

1. Trello

Trello is a project management tool that enables remote teams to manage tasks and workflows effectively. It provides a visual interface that enables team members to see task status, deadlines, and dependencies.

2. Slack

Slack is an instant messaging tool that provides a platform for quick and informal conversations between team members. It supports audio and video calls, file sharing and integrates with other applications like Trello, Google Drive and Dropbox.

3. Zoom

Zoom is a video conferencing tool that provides a platform for remote team members to hold virtual meetings and webinars. It supports screen sharing, breakout rooms, and virtual backgrounds, among other features.

4. Google Drive

Google Drive is a cloud-based solution that provides remote teams with a platform to store, share, and collaborate on files. It facilitates seamless collaboration, version control, and real-time commenting.

Overcoming Challenges of Remote Collaboration

Remote collaboration poses unique challenges that teams must address to foster effective communication, teamwork, and a positive work culture. Below are some challenges of remote collaboration and strategies for overcoming them:

1. Lack of trust

Distance can lead to a lack of trust, which can hinder effective collaboration. Building trust requires effective communication, staying true to commitments, and being transparent and accountable.

2. Time differences

Time differences are a significant challenge for remote collaboration. Teams must find effective ways to coordinate meeting times and deadlines to accommodate members in different time zones.

3. Misunderstandings

Misunderstandings can occur easily in remote collaboration when team members have different cultural backgrounds or language barriers. Effective communication through clear and concise messages, using simple language, and avoiding jargon is critical in overcoming misunderstandings.

Building Teamwork and Positive Work Culture

Building a positive work culture is crucial for remote teams to succeed. Teamwork and camaraderie help foster motivation, collaboration, and accountability, which are all essential ingredients for success. Below are some strategies for building teamwork and a positive work culture in remote teams:

1. Regular virtual team meetings

Regular virtual team meetings help foster camaraderie and help team members feel connected. The meetings provide an opportunity for team members to discuss successes, challenges, and upcoming milestones.

2. Virtual team building activities

Virtual team building activities help build camaraderie and encourage teamwork. These activities can range from virtual games and challenges, virtual happy hours, and online book clubs.

3. Celebrating successes

Successes should be celebrated to build morale and to recognize team members' contributions. Celebrating successes could involve calling out team members' contributions, posting success stories on social media and sending virtual thank-you messages.

Measuring the Effectiveness of Remote Collaboration

Measuring the effectiveness of remote collaboration is critical to ensuring continuous improvement. Below are some metrics that remote teams could use to measure the effectiveness of remote collaboration:

1. Meeting attendance and participation

Attendance and participation levels provide insight into the effectiveness of communication channels within the remote team.

2. Project progress

Tracking project progress helps remote teams identify bottlenecks, adjust workflows, and identify areas of improvement.

3. Feedback from team members

Feedback from team members can provide insight into the effectiveness of collaboration tools and workflows. Regular feedback sessions can help remote teams make adjustments to improve collaboration.

Conclusion

Effective remote collaboration is critical for remote teams to achieve their goals. Remote collaboration involves clear communication, teamwork, and a positive work culture. Remote teams must identify unique challenges of collaboration and strategies to overcome them. Effective collaborations require building trust amongst team members, regular communication, and celebrating successes. Remote collaboration can be measured effectively using metrics such as meeting attendance, project progress, and team member feedback. Remote teams that embrace the importance of collaboration in a remote working environment are more likely to thrive and achieve their objectives.

CHAPTER 7:
REMOTE WORK AND
RECRUITMENT

Remote working has become one of the most significant innovations in the world of work in recent years. Increasingly, organizations are using remote working arrangements as a way to attract and retain top talent in an increasingly competitive marketplace. Remote working arrangements offer businesses the ability to access the best talent, regardless of location, and provide employees with the flexibility to work from anywhere.

In this chapter, we will explore the impact of remote working on recruitment, how organizations can attract top talent with remote work opportunities, and best practices for managing remote employees.

The Impact of Remote Working on Recruitment

Remote working has had a significant impact on recruitment, shifting the focus from location-based hiring to skills-based hiring. Remote work allows organizations to hire the best talent from anywhere in the world, increasing the pool of available candidates and providing more diverse and varied skill sets.

Remote work arrangements also offer businesses the ability to retain talented employees who may have personal or family commitments that may prevent them from relocating. By offering remote work opportunities, employers can meet the needs of their employees while maintaining a productive workforce.

Attracting Top Talent with Remote Work Opportunities

Remote working arrangements have become an important consideration for job seekers, with many candidates prioritizing flexible work arrangements over traditional office-based work. To attract top talent with remote work opportunities, organizations need to develop a strong employer brand, offering employee-centered policies and practices that prioritize work-life balance and support employee well-being.

Employers can also leverage technology and social media to reach a wider pool of candidates. Networking and recruiting platforms like LinkedIn, Twitter, and Glassdoor provide organizations with the resources to create a strong online presence, generating interest in remote work opportunities and showcasing the value of work flexibility.

Assessing Candidates for Remote Work Suitability

Assessing the suitability of candidates for remote work requires organizations to shift their focus from traditional hiring criteria to skills and aptitudes that are essential for remote work success. Hiring managers need to develop a deep understanding of the nuances and intricacies of remote work, including the importance of self-motivation and self-discipline, communication skills, and adaptability.

To assess whether a candidate is suitable for remote work, employers can incorporate behavioral interviews and assessments into their recruitment process. These assessments can help to identify the key competencies required for remote work and assess the candidate's ability to work independently, troubleshoot problems, and maintain a high level of productivity.

Onboarding and Training Remote Employees

Onboarding and training remote employees require careful planning and preparation, ensuring that new hires have the skills and knowledge required to be productive and successful in their new roles. Onboarding should include an introduction to the organization and its culture, clear communication of job expectations and responsibilities, and training on the tools and technologies required for remote work success.

To ensure successful onboarding and training, organizations can leverage technology to provide remote support and resources. This can include virtual training sessions, online learning resources, and mentorship and coaching programs.

Building Trust in Remote Work Relationships

Building trust in remote work relationships is essential to remote work success, requiring personal accountability, effective communication, and strong relationships between managers and employees. Managers must provide clear guidance and support, setting expectations for remote work performance and maintaining regular communication with employees.

Effective communication is particularly important for building trust in remote work environments, enabling managers to provide feedback and support, establish clear expectations, and foster strong community and collaboration. The use of video conferencing, instant messaging, and collaboration tools can support remote work relationships, providing remote workers with the opportunity to connect, collaborate, and build relationships with colleagues.

Managing Employee Expectations in Remote Work Settings

Managing employee expectations in remote work settings

requires an informed and proactive approach, providing employees with the information and support required to succeed in their roles. Setting clear expectations for remote work outcomes and providing regular feedback is essential to reinforcing the importance of the employee's contributions to the organization.

To manage employee expectations, employers can establish clear policies and procedures, providing employees with guidelines for remote work performance, communication, and accountability. Regular check-ins and opportunities for feedback and support can help to address employee concerns and build a culture of mutual respect and trust.

Conclusion

Remote working has transformed the world of work by providing employees with the flexibility to work from anywhere and employers with access to the best talent worldwide. Successful remote work requires an informed and proactive approach, focusing on skills-based hiring, effective communication, and collaboration tools, and building trust and accountability in remote work relationships.

To attract top talent with remote work opportunities, organizations must prioritize employee-centered policies and practices that prioritize work-life balance and support employee well-being. Assessing the suitability of candidates for remote work requires employers to identify key competencies required for remote work success and assess candidate's ability to work independently, troubleshoot problems, and maintain high levels of productivity.

Onboarding and training remote workers require careful planning and preparation, leveraging technology to provide remote support and resources. Building trust in remote work relationships requires personal accountability, effective communication, and strong relationships between managers and employees. Finally, managing employee expectations in remote work settings requires an informed and proactive approach, providing employees with the information and support required to succeed in their roles.

CHAPTER 8: REMOTE WORK AND CYBERSECURITY

As remote work becomes an increasingly popular option for businesses, it is important for employers and employees to be aware of the potential cybersecurity risks that come with working remotely. Cybersecurity risks can impact not only individual remote workers but also the organizations that they work for. In this chapter, we will discuss the risks involved in remote work environments and provide tips and best practices for ensuring cybersecurity.

Cybersecurity Risks in Remote Work Environments

One of the most significant cybersecurity risks in remote work environments is the possibility of a data breach. Since remote workers typically do not have the same level of network security as an office environment, they can be more vulnerable to cyber-attacks. Hackers can exploit security weaknesses in the remote worker's connection to access sensitive data such as customer information, intellectual property, and financial data.

Another risk is the use of unsecured public Wi-Fi networks. It is not uncommon for remote workers to use public Wi-Fi networks such as those at coffee shops, airports, and other public places to complete their tasks. However, these networks are often unsecured and may be easily compromised by hackers.

Phishing scams are also a significant risk in remote work environments. Phishing scams usually involve tricking an individual into revealing sensitive information via email, phone calls, or direct messages on social media channels. These scams can compromise critical data and cause serious financial harm if individuals are not careful.

Best Practices for Ensuring Remote Work Cybersecurity

To ensure cybersecurity in remote work environments, here are some best practices that remote workers should follow:

❖ Use secure networks - Remote employees should avoid using public Wi-Fi networks and instead work on secure, password-protected networks. Using a virtual private network (VPN) is an excellent way to secure internet connections and maintain network privacy.

❖ Use strong passwords and two-factor authentication - Remote workers should utilize strong passwords, use unique passwords for each login, and enable two-factor authentication wherever possible.

❖ Secure devices - All devices used for work should have up-to-date antivirus and anti-malware software installed, and the software should be regularly updated and scanned for potential threats.

❖ Educate employees about cybersecurity best practices - Businesses should educate their remote employees about cybersecurity best practices to reduce the likelihood of employees falling for phishing scams or other attempts to steal sensitive data.

❖ Secure and encrypt sensitive data - Remote workers should ensure that they are using encrypted connections to transfer sensitive data; this will help protect data from potential security breaches.

❖ Have a response plan - Employers and employees should have a response plan in place in case a security breach occurs. All remote workers must know how to report security issues and follow the guidelines set forth in the response plan.

The Role of IT in Remote Work Cybersecurity

IT plays a critical role in ensuring the cybersecurity of remote work environments. It is the responsibility of the IT department to provide remote employees with secure access to corporate networks and ensure that remote workers have the necessary security hardware and software to comply with corporate security policies.

IT departments must also have systems in place to monitor remote workers' activity and ensure that policies are being adhered to. This includes ensuring that software and operating systems are updated regularly to prevent hackers from exploiting vulnerabilities.

Final Thoughts

As remote work continues to gain popularity, cybersecurity risks must be taken seriously. Remote workers must be aware of the potential risks involved in working remotely, and businesses must be equipped to provide secure access to corporate networks. By following best practices in remote work cybersecurity, businesses can create a safe and productive environment for remote workers.

CHAPTER 9: REMOTE WORK AND LEGAL CONSIDERATIONS

Remote work arrangements come with multiple legal considerations that need to be addressed by organizations, especially in the current digital age. Whether you are planning to shift to a remote work model, or are already managing a remote team, legal considerations are critical to ensure compliance with applicable labor laws and regulations. In this chapter, we will explore some essential legal factors to consider while managing remote workers.

Compliance with Labor Laws and Regulations

The first and foremost thing to consider while managing remote workers is compliance with labor laws and regulations. Each country and state have their own set of regulations that cover areas such as minimum wage, working hours, work breaks, insurance policies, and more. Companies must be aware of the labor laws and regulations that are applicable in the jurisdictions where their remote employees reside. Non-compliance with regulations can lead to legal and financial consequences.

Ensuring Employee Safety in Remote Work Settings

Organizations must ensure their remote employees have a

safe workspace at home with minimum hazards. They must have documentation and policies in place to ensure that their remote workers understand safety requirements and follow them accordingly. Companies can conduct safety inspections at an employee's remote workspace to ensure they have adequate ergonomic furniture to avoid potential work-related injuries.

Contractual Agreements for Remote Workers

Companies must have a detailed contractual agreement that outlines the terms and conditions of remote work arrangements. This contract should include employment terms, the scope of work, intellectual property clauses, compensation measures, confidentiality policies, data protection policies, and more. This contract should be drafted in a way that is compliant with labor laws and should be sent to prospective remote workers to review before they start working.

Worker Classification and Tax Considerations

Companies should classify remote workers as either employees or independent contractors to abide by specific labor laws and tax regulations prescribed by the regulatory authorities. If a company is working with independent contractors who reside outside the United States, they will need to comply with different tax regulations of their country.

Protecting Intellectual Property in Remote Work Environments

Intellectual property protection becomes critical when companies have remote workers who access proprietary information systems outside of their office premises. Companies must have robust data access restrictions to keep critical information secure. They should also have confidentiality agreements in place, explicitly mentioning the legal protections available in case of information breaches in case of personal devices.

Litigation and Dispute Resolution in Remote Work Arrangements

Remote work arrangements may lead to conflicts and disputes between the employer and employees, which can result in litigation. Companies must have dispute resolution policies in place that detail the process for raising complaints and the resolution mechanisms. Also, companies should ensure that the contractual agreement clearly outlines the jurisdiction for dispute resolution.

International Legal Considerations for Remote Work

Suppose your company hires remote workers who live in other countries or operate from different time zones. In that case, it is essential to have an understanding of the legal and cultural differences prevailing in the employees' country. For example, employees' leave entitlements, compensation schemes, and employment termination procedures can vary based on the regulations in the country the employee resides in.

In conclusion, companies that choose to work in remote environments require a deep understanding of legal considerations that come with managing remote workers. It is imperative to ensure compliance with applicable labor laws, regulations, and tax schemes while providing safe and secure workspaces. Companies must also have a robust dispute resolution mechanism in place to resolve conflicts between employees and employers. By dealing with legal considerations with the utmost care, employers can maintain a secure, efficient, and robust remote work environment for their employees.

CHAPTER 10: REMOTE WORK AND LEADERSHIP

The world of work is evolving at a rapid pace, with remote work becoming more commonplace than ever before. With such a significant shift in how teams operate, leaders face new challenges in managing their remote teams and ensuring they are producing the desired outcomes. In this chapter, we will explore the unique challenges that remote work poses to leaders and strategies they can use to manage remote teams effectively.

Building Trust and Accountability in Remote Work Teams

Leaders must build trust with their remote teams through clear and transparent communication. Without the opportunity to meet face-to-face, remote workers may feel isolated, unacknowledged, and unappreciated. Leaders must, therefore, ensure they maintain constant communication with their teams and keep a clear line of sight on each employee's progress. Leaders should make it a priority to give feedback often and provide regular opportunities for their remote workers to give feedback.

Managers must also emphasize accountability among their remote teams. As remote employees work independently, they must feel accountable both for meeting performance expectations and adhering to established business protocols and organizational values. To facilitate this, leaders can use performance metrics, measure output, and encourage a sense of ownership amongst remote employees. This way, remote workers remain motivated to meet and even exceed performance expectations.

Managing Performance and Productivity Remotely

As remote work is based on outcomes rather than hours spent at work, leaders must measure the performance of their remote teams differently. Instead of tracking time spent at work, managers should measure output and monitor performance based on established project benchmarks and productivity metrics. By focusing on productivity, managers can ensure remote employees are meeting the needs of the business while also enabling flexibility in work schedules and locations.

Leaders must also provide regular performance feedback to improve the performance of their remote teams. With real-time feedback, remote employees receive constructive criticism and suggestions for improvement in real-time, which leads to improved output and work performance overall.

Communicating Expectations and Goals in Remote Work Settings

In remote work settings, leaders must communicate expectations and goals regularly and transparently. This means using clear instructions, checklists, to-do lists, and establishing a regular check-in schedule to discuss work progress with pride. With frequent communication, remote employees will remain informed and understand what they need to do to deliver results. Managers must actively listen to their remote workers and prioritize clear and open communication to avoid any misunderstandings or ambiguity.

Leading Through Change in Remote Work Environments

Remote work is still a relatively new concept for many organizations, and change is an ever-present force, especially with digital and technological disruption in every industry. Managers must display adaptability, flexibility, responsiveness, and creativity to enact change effectively in remote work environments. This requires introducing and leading with new tools, processes, and technologies connected instantly to remote teams.

Developing a Leadership Style for Remote Work Settings

Leaders must focus on developing a leadership style tailored to remote work settings. Leaders must be authentic, transparent, and forward-thinking in their leadership approach. This means focusing on connection-building and promoting trust amongst the remote team, fostering a culture of inclusivity, building flexibility into work schedules to promote employee work-life balance, tapping into the individual strengths of remote employees, and promoting active collaboration amongst team members.

Strategies for Motivating and Engaging Remote Work Teams

Leaders must focus on engaging and motivating remote workers effectively. Instead of fixed schedules and performance-based incentives, remote workers require personalized approaches. Few examples of motivators include growth opportunities, job satisfaction, increased autonomy in work, and higher rates of task variety. Leaders must leverage these motivators while simultaneously creating a sense of community to keep their remote teams engaged, connected, and motivated.

Overcoming Challenges in Remote Work Leadership

Remote work leadership requires proactively addressing the unique challenges in this form of work. With no physical presence to monitor their remote teams, leaders must trust and rely on their employees to get their work done. Managers must establish trust with their remote teams while also implementing performance metrics to help bring accountability and clarity to the work produced. Leaders must also establish clear communication channels to allow remote employees to feel connected to the larger purpose of the organization and prioritize building trust.

Conclusion

Remote work presents unique challenges for leaders, but with preparation, intentionality, and a personal touch, these challenges can be overcome. With clear communication, performance metrics, and personalized strategies to maintain team engagement and motivation, remote teams can be managed successfully. The future of work is remote, and the potential for growth and productivity is vast, making it essential for leaders to develop and hone the skills and strategies needed to lead their teams into the future of work.

CHAPTER 11: REMOTE WORK AND PROJECT MANAGEMENT

The recent pandemic has forced many businesses to adopt remote work practices, which have turned out to be successful for many companies. One of the most important aspects of remote working is project management, which entails coordinating and managing resources to achieve a specific goal within a specified time frame. As such, project management is critical for businesses that want to maintain efficiency, productivity, and profitability while operating remotely. This chapter will discuss the best practices in remote project management to help organizations achieve their goals while working remotely.

Effective project management requires clear communication, proper planning, and the use of the right tools. While these elements are important regardless of the work setting, they become even more critical in remote work environments, where team members must work together to achieve a common objective while located in different parts of the world. As such, remote project management requires managers to embrace a more collaborative approach to managing workflows and resources.

When it comes to communication, remote project managers must strive for clarity, transparency, and consistency. They should maintain regular communication with their teams, creating an environment where everyone knows what is expected of them and what is going on with the project. Communication can be done through tools such as email, chat applications, and video conferencing. It is also essential to establish guidelines and protocols for communication to ensure that everyone understands the expectations and structure.

Proper planning is also an important aspect of remote project management. Project managers should develop detailed project plans that outline specific tasks, timelines, and resources required to achieve the project's objectives. Planning ahead helps to keep team members on track and prevents the need to backtrack or make adjustments during the project that can cause delays. Furthermore, project managers should ensure that team members have access to the tools and resources they need to carry out their tasks without delays.

Another critical aspect of remote project management is the use of the right tools and technologies. There are various project management tools available in the market, including Trello, Asana, and Basecamp. These tools are designed to simplify workflows, track progress, and provide an intuitive interface for team members to collaborate on projects. The tools also help managers to monitor the project's progress and identify potential bottlenecks early.

Managing timelines and deadlines can be particularly challenging in remote project management. Managers need to communicate with team members to ensure that everyone understands the timelines and deadlines for different tasks so that they can plan accordingly. Where possible, managers should allow for some flexibility in the deadlines to accommodate unexpected issues that may arise during the project.

Team collaboration remains a crucial factor in remote project management success. Managers must create an environment where team members can work together to achieve common goals. They should ensure that team members have access to each other, including tools and platforms for online meetings, collaborative messaging, and joint editing of documents. Additionally, project managers should create project-specific workflows so that team members can collaborate seamlessly, share knowledge, and interact with ease.

Measuring project success is essential in remote project management. Managers should track the project's progress at different stages to identify potential issues and take corrective action as required. Performance metrics should be established to help managers evaluate the project's performance and identify areas for improvement.

Challenges are bound to arise in remote project management, just like any other project implementation. Managers should be prepared to address any issues that come up, which may include delays, unexpected changes, and technical glitches. In such cases, developing contingency plans, assigning responsibilities, and communicating effectively are critical to minimizing the impact of the issues.

Ultimately, successful remote project management requires managers to recognize the unique nature of remote work environments and adapt their strategies to create successful project outcomes. Embracing new tools, technologies, and communication techniques are the keys to managing remote projects effectively. With proper planning, coordination, and execution, remote project management can be as successful as traditional project management, achieving objectives, improving efficiencies, and generating business growth.

CHAPTER 12: REMOTE WORK AND PERFORMANCE MANAGEMENT

Performance management is an essential aspect of any organization, as it drives productivity and results. In remote work arrangements, managing employee performance can be challenging, especially when it comes to setting expectations, providing feedback, and assessing progress.

Setting Performance Expectations

Setting realistic and measurable performance expectations for remote workers is critical to ensure that they understand what is expected of them. Managers must collaborate with their remote employees to develop individual performance goals that are aligned with the organization's objectives. The performance goals should clearly articulate what are the expected deliverables, milestones, timelines, and quality standards. Remote workers need to have a clear understanding of the performance expectations and how it will be assessed and rewarded.

Providing Feedback and Coaching to Remote Employees

Providing timely and constructive feedback is a key aspect

of performance management that managers must prioritize in remote work settings. Feedback and coaching help remote workers understand how they are progressing towards their performance goals and what specific actions they need to take to improve. The feedback should be specific, actionable, and tied to the performance expectations set for the individual. Offering feedback on a regular basis through video calls, instant messages, or emails can help to ensure that remote workers stay engaged and motivated.

Measuring and Assessing Remote Worker Performance

Measuring and assessing remote worker performance can be challenging due to the lack of visibility and interaction that managers have with their remote employees. To track performance, managers need to rely on data-driven metrics, such as time tracking, productivity tracking, and software performance analytics. These metrics can help managers to assess whether the individual's performance is meeting the performance expectations and identify areas that require improvement.

Overcoming Challenges in Managing Remote Worker Performance

Managing remote worker performance can present challenges such as communication barriers, cultural differences, and time zones. To address these challenges, managers need to ensure that they use effective communication strategies, leverage technology tools and resources, and establish clear expectations and boundaries. It is equally important to invest in the professional development of remote workers, provide them with training opportunities, and create a culture of continuous learning.

The Impact of Remote Work on Employee Engagement and Motivation

Remote work arrangements can have a significant impact on employee engagement and motivation. Remote workers may feel disconnected from their colleagues and the organization, leading to a lack of engagement and motivation. To improve engagement and motivation, managers need to create a positive remote work environment that fosters collaboration, social interaction, and a sense of belonging. Managers should also recognize and reward the efforts and achievements of remote workers to help build their motivation and commitment.

Developing a Performance Management Strategy for Remote Work

To effectively manage remote worker performance, managers need to develop a performance management strategy that is tailored to the unique needs and challenges of remote work environments. The strategy should include clear guidelines on setting performance expectations, providing feedback and coaching, measuring and assessing performance, and addressing performance issues. The strategy should also align with the organization's overall performance management philosophy and priorities.

Conclusion

Managing employee performance is critical to the success of any organization, and remote work arrangements present unique challenges in this area. To effectively manage remote worker performance, managers must develop a performance management strategy that addresses the challenges of remote work environments. This includes setting realistic performance expectations, providing timely feedback and coaching, measuring and assessing performance, and recognizing and rewarding accomplishments. By implementing a robust performance management strategy, organizations can optimize their remote workers' performance and drive business results.

CHAPTER 13:
REMOTE WORK AND DIVERSITY, EQUITY, AND INCLUSION (DEI)

Diversity, equity, and inclusion (DEI) are critical considerations in the business world. However, with remote work arrangements, there are unique challenges in achieving DEI goals. This chapter examines the impact of remote work on DEI and strategies for promoting diversity, equity, and inclusion in remote work environments.

DEI Considerations in Remote Work Environments

Remote work arrangements have the potential to foster diversity and inclusivity by eliminating location-based biases. Remote work options enable businesses to hire employees from different regions, cultures, and backgrounds, giving diverse perspectives and experiences. Compared to traditional work environments, remote work arrangements promote inclusivity for various reasons:

❖ The remote work environment is more flexible, allowing employees to design their work experience based on their preferences and needs.

❖ Remote work embraces an autonomous work culture, allowing employees to control their responsibilities and timelines, leading to better work-life balance and reduced burnout.

❖ It promotes a self-managing work environment for employees, empowering them to be accountable for their contribution to the company.

However, despite these benefits, remote work arrangements also present unique challenges to DEI. For example, remote work settings can promote a sense of isolation and disconnection from the company culture and peers, which increases the risk of employee exclusion and loneliness. Additionally, the remote work environment may not accommodate cultural expressions for employees, leading to biases and exclusion.

Achieving Diversity and Inclusion in Remote Work Settings

Promoting DEI in remote work settings requires proactive measures to create an inclusive environment for all employees. Here are strategies for achieving diversity and inclusion in remote work settings:

1. Create Inclusive Communication Channels and Environments

Remote work environments require companies to shift their communication methods; companies should facilitate open, accessible, and inclusive communication channels. This includes regular team dialogs, virtual chit-chats and check-ins, and surveys to gauge employee satisfaction.

2. Build a Transparent and Inclusive Recruitment Process

Remote work arrangements offer employers an opportunity for recruiting from a larger pool of talent without the limitations of location. To achieve diversity in remote work settings, companies must create unbiased recruitment practices; this includes advertising job vacancies to a diverse pool of candidates as well as training hiring managers on DEI.

3. Provide DEI Awareness and Training

Providing DEI awareness and training is critical for empowering remote workers and fostering inclusivity. It includes providing adequate support for employees to learn and develop their cultural competency, self-awareness, and unconscious bias.

4. Establish Clear and Inclusive Company Policies

Developing policies that promote diversity and inclusion in remote work environments communicates the company commitment to DEI to all employees. It includes fair policies that promote employee wellbeing, work-life balance, and adequate feedback mechanisms to address workplace issues.

5. Develop a Culture of Inclusivity

Developing a remote work culture that values diversity and inclusivity encourages employees to bring their whole selves to work. This includes creating a welcoming and inclusive work environment by recognizing employee achievements, encouraging expression of different cultures, and supporting community-based projects.

Measuring and Assessing the Effectiveness of DEI in Remote Work

DEI strategies in remote work must include continuous monitoring and assessment to measure effectiveness and identify areas for improvement. It includes gathering feedback from employees, using metrics to track progress on diversity and inclusivity, and celebrating success stories.

Conclusion

DEI is no longer an optional component of remote workplaces. The potential benefits of DEI in remote work environments, are significant, including improved employee satisfaction, engagement, and better overall results. However, addressing the challenges that come with ensuring diversity and inclusivity in remote workspaces is a complex task, requiring constant monitoring and proactive measures. Companies that prioritize DEI in remote work environments are better positioned to remain competitive and prepared for the future.

CHAPTER 14: REMOTE WORK AND ENTREPRENEURSHIP

Entrepreneurship has traditionally been associated with the idea of starting a business within a brick-and-mortar location. However, with the growing popularity of remote work, entrepreneurs are beginning to realize that they can run a successful business entirely from home. Remote work has opened up new frontiers for entrepreneurs, making it easier than ever to reach a global audience and pursue their business dreams. This chapter explores the benefits of entrepreneurship in remote work environments and provides strategies for starting a remote business.

Building a Business through Remote Work Opportunities

Remote work presents numerous opportunities for entrepreneurs looking to build a business. One of the main advantages of remote work is its flexibility, which allows entrepreneurs to work from any location and tailor their work schedule to their needs. This provides entrepreneurs with the freedom to pursue their business goals while also juggling other responsibilities, such as caring for children or elderly parents.

Remote work also presents a range of cost-saving benefits, which can be particularly attractive to entrepreneurs just starting out. Remote work eliminates the need to rent office space, reducing costs associated with overhead, utilities, and furniture. Additionally, remote work minimizes travel costs, as entrepreneurs can easily communicate with clients and employees from anywhere in the world.

Benefits and Drawbacks of Remote Entrepreneurship

The benefits of remote entrepreneurship are numerous, but there are drawbacks as well. One of the main challenges of remote entrepreneurship is the lack of face-to-face interaction with clients and employees. This can make it more difficult to establish trust and build relationships, particularly in the early stages of the business.

Another challenge of remote entrepreneurship is the lack of structure and support. Entrepreneurship can be a lonely pursuit, and without the structure and support of a traditional office environment, it can be easy to lose focus and motivation. However, these challenges can be overcome with the right strategies and resources.

Strategies for Starting and Growing a Remote Business

Starting and growing a remote business requires a different set of strategies than traditional brick-and-mortar businesses. One of the first steps in starting a remote business is to establish a strong online presence. This can be achieved through social media, blogs, and websites that showcase the entrepreneur's products and services.

Another important strategy is to cultivate a network of like-minded individuals and businesses. This can be achieved through networking events, online forums, or partnerships with complementary businesses. Building relationships early on can provide invaluable support and opportunities for collaboration down the line.

In addition to these strategies, entrepreneurs should also prioritize developing strong communication skills. Communication is essential in remote work environments, and entrepreneurs should be comfortable using a range of communication tools and technologies to collaborate with clients and employees.

Overcoming Challenges in Remote Entrepreneurship

Remote entrepreneurship presents its share of challenges, but with the right strategies, entrepreneurs can overcome these obstacles and build a successful business. One of the biggest challenges entrepreneurs face is managing their time effectively. Remote work environments can be full of distractions, and entrepreneurs should prioritize creating a workspace conducive to productivity and minimizing distractions.

Another challenge is staying motivated and focused. Entrepreneurship can be a lonely pursuit, and without the structure and accountability of a traditional office environment, it can be easy to lose motivation. However, entrepreneurs can combat this by setting clear goals and deadlines, establishing a regular routine, and seeking out like-minded individuals for support and inspiration.

The Future of Remote Work and Entrepreneurship

Remote work presents numerous opportunities for entrepreneurs looking to start or grow a business. As remote work grows in popularity, entrepreneurs will continue to discover new ways to leverage this flexible approach to work to achieve their business goals. The future of remote entrepreneurship is bright, and entrepreneurs who embrace this growing trend will be well-positioned for success.

CHAPTER 15: REMOTE WORK AND EDUCATION

The pandemic has accelerated the trend towards remote learning and education. Traditional classroom settings have been disrupted by the pandemic, forcing millions of students to transition to remote learning environments. Remote education is not a new concept, but it has gained popularity in the past few years due to advancements in technology and the need for more flexible education options. In this chapter, we will discuss the impact of remote working on education, the benefits and drawbacks of remote learning, strategies for effective remote teaching and learning, tools and technologies for remote education, measuring and assessing the effectiveness of remote education, overcoming challenges in remote education, and finally, the future of remote education.

Impact of Remote Working on Education

Remote working has had a significant impact on education. The pandemic has forced schools and universities to shift from traditional in-person classrooms to remote learning environments. This has meant that students and educators have had to rely on technology to continue their studies. While remote learning has its challenges, it has opened up opportunities for students who may not have been able to attend traditional in-person classrooms due to various reasons like distance, disability, or family commitments.

Benefits and Drawbacks of Remote Learning

Remote learning has several benefits. One of the main advantages is the flexibility it offers as students can study at their own pace and on their own schedule. The use of technology has made remote learning more interactive and engaging. Remote learning has also made education accessible to a wider audience, regardless of geographical location.

However, remote learning comes with its own set of drawbacks. One of the main concerns is the lack of social interactions between students and teachers. Remote learning can also lead to isolation and a lack of motivation among students. Many students have also reported that it is difficult to concentrate on their studies while at home.

Strategies for Effective Remote Teaching and Learning

To ensure effective remote teaching and learning, instructors need to adjust their teaching methods to the remote environment. The following strategies can be used for effective remote teaching:

❖ Active learning: Instructors should focus on active learning and design lessons that promote participation and engagement.

❖ Synchronous and asynchronous learning: Instructors should include both synchronous and asynchronous learning in their teaching methods.

❖ Interactivity: Instructors should incorporate interactive tools and technologies to create engaging learning experiences.

❖ Communication: Instructors should ensure regular

communication with their students to address their concerns and provide feedback.

Tools and Technologies for Remote Education

Technology plays a crucial role in remote education. The following tools and technologies can be used for effective remote education:

- ❖ Learning Management Systems (LMS): An LMS is a software platform used by educators to manage and deliver educational content.

- ❖ Video Conferencing: Video conferencing tools like Zoom, Google Meet, and Microsoft Teams are used for synchronous remote learning sessions.

- ❖ Content Creation Tools: Content creation tools like Camtasia and Adobe Captivate can be used to create engaging educational content.

- ❖ Cloud Storage: Cloud storage services like Dropbox and Google Drive can be used to store and share educational materials.

Measuring and Assessing the Effectiveness of Remote Education

Assessing the effectiveness of remote education is crucial. Educators should focus on the following metrics:

- ❖ Student Engagement: Educators should measure student engagement through participation rates, feedback, and assessments.

- ❖ Knowledge Retention: Educators should assess the effectiveness of remote learning by measuring knowledge retention rates.

- ❖ Student Satisfaction: Educators should gather feedback

from students to assess their satisfaction with the remote learning experience.

Overcoming Challenges in Remote Education

The challenges in remote education can be overcome by incorporating the following practices:

- ❖ Regular Communication: Regular communication between educators and students can help in addressing concerns and providing support.

- ❖ Clear Expectations: Educators should set clear learning objectives and expectations for their students.

- ❖ Structured Learning: A structured learning experience can help students stay on track and motivated.

The Future of Remote Education

Remote education is here to stay, and its popularity is likely to grow in the coming years. The use of technology in education will continue to advance, making remote education more engaging and effective. The future of remote education will also see an increase in flexibility, allowing students to learn at their own pace and on their schedules. As the world continues to change, remote education will adapt to meet the needs of students and educators alike.

Conclusion

Remote education has become an essential aspect of learning in the wake of the COVID-19 pandemic. While remote learning comes with its own set of challenges, the benefits are significant. Remote education offers flexibility, accessibility, and interactivity, making it an effective alternative to traditional classroom learning. It is vital for educators to adapt their teaching methods to the remote environment effectively. The use of technology and regular communication can help overcome the challenges in remote education. The future of remote education is bright, and it will continue to grow and evolve to meet the needs of students and educators.

CHAPTER 16: REMOTE WORK AND MENTAL HEALTH

The global pandemic has led to an unprecedented increase in remote work arrangements, and while this has come with its benefits, it has also brought about a number of challenges, including mental health concerns. Remote work can affect mental health in both positive and negative ways, and it's essential for individuals, companies, and leaders to recognize and address these issues as they arise.

Mental health considerations in remote work environments

Remote work arrangements can take a toll on an individual's mental health. One of the main issues is the lack of social interaction as workers may feel isolated and disconnected from their colleagues. Feelings of loneliness can increase, and it can lead to unaddressed mental health issues. This is particularly true for individuals who live alone or for those who do not have a designated work area at home. It is also possible that remote workers feel more pressure from their responsibilities at work. This could be due to blurred lines between work and home responsibilities when working remotely. There is a risk of employees becoming overworked and mentally strained from having to navigate through their responsibilities. Remote workers are also likely to experience more stress because the work environment is always available. It is important for workers to have a work-life balance even when working remotely.

Strategies for promoting mental health in remote work settings

The challenges in remote work arrangements should be addressed by promoting mental health. Here are some strategies to promote mental health among remote workers:

❖ Encourage social interaction: Social isolation is often a common problem in remote work settings. Leaders should encourage remote workers to connect with their colleagues through video conferencing, messaging apps, or phone calls. Team building activities should also be organized at least once a month to encourage collaboration and interaction.

❖ Create a supportive work culture: The work environment should prioritize support for the employees. Leaders and co-workers should be encouraged to check in on each other frequently to gauge their mental wellbeing.

❖ Establish boundaries: Workers should establish working schedules and stick to them. Working remotely does not mean that employees need to work non-stop. It is important to have time to disconnect from work and their screens.

❖ Promote healthy lifestyles: Remote workers should be encouraged to engage in wellness activities such as yoga, exercise, or aerobic workout sessions after work hours to maintain a healthy lifestyle.

❖ Encourage breaks: Encouraging break times can also boost productivity and prevent burnout incidences. A ten-minute break to walk around or stretch every hour is an effective way of preventing eye strain and neck or back pain.

Identifying and addressing mental health issues in remote

workers

Leaders in remote work settings should also be able to recognize when their employees are having mental health issues and address them appropriately. Here's how:

❖ Be attentive to mood changes: If a remote worker starts struggling, their work performance may suffer. Employees may also display a change of behavior different from their typical demeanor. Leaders should look out for these changes and address them as they occur.

❖ Encourage open communication: Remote workers should feel valued by their leaders and be able to reach out to request accommodation or to discuss their concerns.

❖ Provide support resources: It is important to give employees access to confidential services through a trusted employee assistance program (EAP) service provider. This can provide employee counselling services and other resources.

The future of remote work and mental health

The future of remote work seems to be promising. Companies that are shifting to remote work have continued to see cost-saving benefits, and employees have enjoyed a flexible working environment. Mental health will be an important aspect of remote work as it is becoming a priority for organizations and individuals. Leaders, employees, and companies can develop strategies to address mental health concerns in remote work settings. The pandemic has forced many workers across the world to work remotely, and the benefits, challenges, and mental health concerns in remote work have been magnified. As more companies have made the decision to continue with remote work arrangements, mental health issues will become increasingly important. Therefore, it is essential to prioritize the mental wellbeing of remote workers in the future.

Conclusion

Remote work is the future of work, and it's important for both employees and employers to recognize its benefits as well as the challenges it can bring, particularly when it comes to mental health. Remote work can positively affect mental health with flexible schedules and a supportive work culture. However, it is important for organizations to recognize when mental health issues arise and address them accordingly. Mental health can be promoted through effective communication, social interaction, establishing boundaries, promoting healthy lifestyles, and taking breaks. Remote work is the future, and leaders, employees, and organizations need to prioritize mental health to reap the full benefits of remote work arrangements.

CHAPTER 17: REMOTE WORK AND SOCIAL RESPONSIBILITY

Remote work has given rise to new opportunities and possibilities for social responsibility, arising from the changes it's made in the traditional workforce. Companies can now not only move towards becoming more environmentally sustainable, but also address social and economic inequalities in an entirely new way. As remote work has become a vital component in industry due to the pandemic, it is important to focus on how remote work can create positive social impact.

Social responsibility in remote work arrangements involves a greater focus on the impact a company has on society and the environment. There is an expectation that corporations and businesses are good citizens in their local communities and care about the welfare of the planet as a whole. Remote work has created a unique opportunity to facilitate such a positive impact on society and the world.

Corporate Social Responsibility in the Remote Work Environment

Corporate Social Responsibility (CSR) refers to the ethical and moral responsibility of corporations towards society, in addition to their financial goals. The principles of CSR include taking responsibility for the impact of business activities on society, safeguarding the environment, treating employees with dignity and respect, and increasing transparency and ethical business practices.

Remote work arrangements in corporations have provided new opportunities for companies to demonstrate their CSR as well as greater scope for it. With more employees working from home, companies can effectively reduce their environmental impact, personalizing their initiatives to meet local needs. For instance, by reducing commuter travel, carbon emissions decrease, reducing air pollution and energy usage. This is also true for companies who adopt remote work arrangements.

Environmental Impact of Remote Work Arrangements

Remote work has a direct impact on the environment that should not be underestimated. It can significantly reduce the carbon footprint of a company if the arrangement is implemented effectively. Cutting back on employee travelling to work leads to fewer cars on the road. Thus, remote work arrangements can significantly reduce energy usage and limit the use of non-renewable fuels.

Many organizations are switching to paperless operations through remote work arrangements. This not only contributes to environmental sustainability, but also saves time and space when it comes to document storage. Recycling and conservation practices can be communicated more easily in remote work environments, which encourages a more sustainable outlook on daily practices.

Addressing Issues of Social and Economic Inequality Through Remote Work Opportunities

Remote work arrangements can help address socio-economic concerns in a world where income inequality continues to widen, and the rise of economic challenges puts a lot of people on the back foot. Remote work gives people access to work opportunities that, in the traditional sense, they might be unable to access, for several reasons, such as location, physical and mental limitations and lack of education.

Remote work simplifies access to the global economy. It means that people in rural areas, small towns and remote areas can be gainfully employed without having to leave their homes. This reduces costs of living and improves quality of life. Remote work also helps the disabled and the elderly enjoy gainful employment opportunities as they are not subjected to time, mobility or other physical constraints.

Remote working is a perfect example of a practical solution that companies can use to address these issues. For example, through outsourcing, companies can provide remote work opportunities to women and minorities who may be discriminated against in the domestic job market. It is also worth mentioning that remote work is not limited to a company's immediate surroundings. It is genuinely a global solution to the social and economic inequalities present worldwide.

Overcoming Challenges in Promoting Social Responsibility in Remote Work Settings

The primary challenge in promoting CSR in remote work environments is to ensure that the impact is meaningful. Even though, the factors of CSR are often viewed as a secondary priority in the face of financial goals, it is important to understand that emphasizing CSR practices is not only beneficial to society and the environment, but it is also beneficial to the company that practices it.

Another challenge is weighing the expectations of the remote workforce who have moved to working from home and have new expectations of work-life balance. Adopting company practices in line with employee expectations and preferences when it comes to social responsibility is a critical balance to maintain and is especially important for attracting and retaining top talent.

There are also some concerns from a legal perspective regarding enforcing social and environmental standards across borders. In managing remote workers, it might be difficult to ensure that they are acting in accordance with the company's guidelines. It's essential that companies are clear in communicating their social responsibility values, mission, and expectations, ensuring they resonate with company employees.

Future of Social Responsibility and Remote Work

The future of remote work demands that corporations embrace social responsibility as a natural factor of doing business. Governments can also play a role in promoting CSR by enacting fiscal policies that encourage social responsibility and environmental sustainability. It is in many ways an achievable business prerogative that helps a company align with ethical principles and meet social expectations, while at the same time, achieving sustainable financial returns.

Remote work is getting more integrated into business practices as people and organizations adapt to the significant changes brought about by COVID-19. The future of CSR in remote work environments entails carefully examining the impact of businesses on the environment, local communities, and society.

It is essential to know that remote work does not interfere with productivity in any way. In fact, companies that promote social responsibility make it their business to use remote work arrangements as a way to contribute to the environment. While investing in social responsibility as an aspect of remote work is the right thing to do, we also understand that it is also what employees expect from forward-thinking organizations.

CHAPTER 18: REMOTE WORK AND FUTURE TRENDS

Remote work has gained significant momentum in the past few years and its growth has been exponential since the pandemic forced organizations to adapt to the new norm of remote work arrangements. This chapter discusses some of the future trends that will shape remote work arrangements and their impact on businesses and workers.

Emerging Trends in Remote Work Arrangements

Several emerging trends will continue to shape remote work arrangements and their impact on the future of work. Some of these trends include:

1. Blended Work Models

With most organizations embracing the hybrid model of remote work, blended work models – which combine physical and virtual offices – are poised to be the future of work. In blended work models, employees can choose to work from either a physical or a virtual office, or a combination of both.

2. The Gig Economy

The gig economy is rapidly expanding, and it will continue to transform the way work is done in the near future. With the rise of freelance job sites like Upwork, Freelancer, and Fiverr, a large workforce of independent professionals now exists, and more organizations are embracing this trend.

3. Virtual Reality and Augmented Reality

The development of virtual and augmented reality technologies is paving the way for the creation of immersive remote work environments. These emerging technologies have the potential to create a shared workspace that mimics a physical environment, fostering efficient collaboration between team members.

4. The Internet of Things (IoT)

The Internet of Things refers to devices – from coffee makers to cars to household appliances – that are connected to the internet. With IoT, it will be possible to work remotely while staying connected to even the most mundane devices.

The Impact of Globalization on Remote Work Opportunities

Globalization has transformed the world with its positive and negative effects on remote work opportunities. It has made it possible for people on opposite ends of the world to work together seamlessly. Remote work has eliminated most geographical barriers and opened up opportunities for individuals to work for companies that they may never have had access to before, regardless of where they are based.

In addition, globalization has facilitated cross-cultural exchange, which enriches the diversity of remote work teams. Remote work allows businesses to access diverse expertise from all over the world, giving them a competitive edge and promoting global cultural understanding.

The Role of Technology in Shaping the Future of Remote Work

Technology has played a key role in the rapid growth of remote work, and it will continue to shape its future. AI-powered communication and collaboration technologies, developments in cloud storage and security, and virtual reality will continue to enhance remote work arrangements. In addition, advanced tools and technologies for remote work productivity management, project management, time tracking, and communication will continue to emerge.

Organizations that invest in the right tools and technologies will gain a competitive advantage over their counterparts and will be better equipped to deal with the challenges and opportunities that remote work offers.

Overcoming Challenges in Adapting to Future Trends in Remote Work

The future of work is uncertain and dynamic, and remote work arrangements must be adaptable and flexible enough to embrace emerging trends. To do so, businesses must take a proactive approach to training their employees on how to use the latest technologies and adapting to new work models. Businesses need to invest in employee training and development to ensure that their remote workforce is capable and equipped to handle future challenges that come with the rapidly evolving digital world.

The Future of Remote Work After the Pandemic

The COVID-19 pandemic has proven that remote work is here to stay. Even when the pandemic subsides, more businesses will continue to embrace remote work practices. The pandemic has increased employer and employee confidence in remote work arrangements and has shown that operating remotely can be a feasible and effective way to work.

Preparing for the Future of Remote Work

Remote work presents a wealth of opportunities for businesses and individuals alike. To realize the benefits that remote work offers, businesses need to develop robust remote work policies, invest in employee skills training, and leverage advanced tools and technologies. To prepare for the future, businesses need to be agile, innovative, and adaptable to change in a fast-paced, technological world.

Conclusion

The future of work is rapidly evolving, and it is increasingly clear that remote work is an integral part of it. Businesses that embrace the potential of remote work, adapt to the latest trends and technology, and develop robust remote work policies, will benefit from improved productivity, a diverse workforce, lower overhead costs, and a more motivated workforce. The future is looking bright for remote work, and businesses that take advantage of this trend have a competitive edge in the global marketplace.

CHAPTER 19: REMOTE WORK AND PERSONAL DEVELOPMENT

Remote working provides individuals with opportunities for personal development and growth in their careers. The flexible nature of remote work allows workers to engage in self-improvement activities that will enhance their skills and competencies. Remote workers can build new skills, gain experience, and explore different paths for their career advancement. In this chapter, we explore the opportunities for personal development in remote work environments, the challenges that come with them, and how to overcome these challenges.

Building skills and competencies in remote work settings:

Remote work environments provide a unique opportunity for workers to build skills and competencies that will be beneficial for their professional growth. Remote work setups require workers to have specific technical skills such as digital literacy, online communication skills, and proficiency in collaboration platforms. Remote work environments also require soft skills such as time-management, self-discipline, and adaptability. These skills can be built through training programs, certification courses, or skill-building exercises that can be done flexibly at the worker's own pace. Remote workers can also take advantage of the various opportunities provided by the employer to hone their skills, attend webinars, and participate in professional development programs.

Opportunities for self-improvement and growth through remote work:

Remote work environments offer several opportunities for self-improvement and personal growth. Remote workers can take advantage of the flexibility of their schedule to take courses, attend seminars, and gain new certifications. They can also network with professionals in their field through online communities, social media, and other virtual platforms. Remote work also offers more autonomy and control over one's workspace, enabling workers to create environments that encourage focus, productivity, and creativity.

The impact of remote work on career growth and advancement:

Remote work arrangements have gradually become a standard option for both employers and employees. The growth of remote work creates more opportunities for remote workers to explore career paths, experience different work cultures, and move up the career ladder. Remote workers can also leverage technology to network with global professionals, broaden their contacts, and showcase their skills and qualifications.

Developing a personal development plan for remote work opportunities:

To take advantage of the opportunities to build skills and advance their careers in remote work environments, it is essential for workers to develop a personal development plan. This plan should identify areas of improvement or skill development that will enhance their work performance and increase their employability. It should include realistic goals, achievable timelines, and an evaluation process to monitor progress. The plan should also consider the resources available for skill building, such as the employer-provided training programs and development opportunities.

Overcoming challenges in personal development in remote work environments:

Though remote work provides significant opportunities for personal development and growth in careers, they come with challenges. Remote workers can experience isolation, lack of motivation, and work-life imbalance that can affect their personal development and career advancement. To overcome the challenges of personal development in remote work environments, remote workers should establish routines that promote productivity, mental health, and work-life balance. They can also network with other remote workers, join professional associations, or participate in online communities to mitigate feelings of isolation.

The future of personal development and remote work:

The growth of remote work in recent years has opened doors to new opportunities for personal development and growth. Technological advancements, globalization, and changing work patterns mean that remote workers need to continuously develop their skills and competencies. Remote workers must adapt to new technologies, professional trends, and work cultures to stay competitive in their fields. As remote work becomes more prevalent, the opportunities for personal development will increase, and employers and employees must continue to invest in professional development.

Conclusion:

Remote work provides ample opportunities for personal

development and growth that can benefit workers' career advancement and employability. Remote workers can build skills and competencies, take advantage of self-improvement opportunities, and leverage technology to network and showcase their abilities. Developing a personal development plan can help remote workers identify areas for improvement, set achievable goals, and evaluate their progress. Remote workers must also overcome the challenges of isolation, motivation, and work-life imbalance to maximize opportunities for personal development. As remote work continues to grow, the opportunities for personal development and growth will continue to increase, and remote workers must be proactive about investing in their professional development.

CHAPTER 20: CONCLUSION

Remote working has become an essential part of today's digital world, it has gained elevated importance. In this book, we presented the benefits of remote work arrangements, ranging from increased productivity and cost savings to enhanced work-life balance and employee satisfaction. Remote work has emerged as a game-changer for businesses during these tough times.

This final chapter concludes our exploration of the remote working world. We summarize the key ideas presented in this book, consider the future of remote work arrangements, and call for businesses and organizations to embrace remote working opportunities.

Future Outlook of Remote Working

Remote working has gained momentum in the present, and in the future, it is likely to revolutionize the way we work. The future of remote work arrangements will be popular, with a growing workforce working from anywhere in the world and growing work opportunities.

Remote work makes it possible to collaborate and communicate virtually. It provides the ability to work and interact with anyone, anywhere, thus helping companies access top talent from around the world. In the future, remote work is going to emerge as a critical component of a business's strategy, providing a range of benefits from increased productivity to employee satisfaction and cost savings.

Call to Action

We have provided numerous benefits to businesses considering implementing remote work arrangements. With everything that we presented, we hope that you have a better understanding of how remote work can be beneficial to your organization.

Our call to action is that businesses must begin planning for remote work arrangements, including developing policies and procedures for remote work, and investing in the appropriate technologies and infrastructure. We hope this book motivates business owners to consider remote work arrangements as an essential part of their company's future.

Final Thoughts

Remote work provides a range of advantages to individuals and business owners. It enables employees to work from wherever they want and helps companies realize the benefits of cost savings, increased productivity, and employee satisfaction. By acknowledging the potential of remote work arrangements, businesses can capitalize on these benefits and explore new opportunities for growth.

I hope you have enjoyed this book and I firmly believe that remote work is the future. By taking the steps outlined in this book, businesses can recognize the potential advantages of remote work arrangements and position themselves for long-term success.

In conclusion, remote working offers many benefits that are hard to ignore. It provides individuals with the flexibility and freedom to work from anywhere in the world, without sacrificing their productivity or quality of work. Remote working eliminates the need for long commutes, stressful office environments, and allows for a better work-life balance.

Moreover, remote workers have more time to invest in hobbies, family activities, and other personal pursuits that enrich their lives outside of work. They don't have to worry about missing important moments because they are stuck in traffic or working late at the office.

As technology continues to advance and more companies adopt a remote workforce model, it is clear that remote working is not just a trend but a new way of life. Its benefits go beyond individual employees as companies can save on overhead costs and benefit from access to a wider pool of talent.

In this book, we have explored the various benefits of remote working and provided practical tips on how to make remote work successful for you. So whether you're an employee seeking more flexibility or an employer looking to expand your workforce options – embrace the power of remote working!

ABOUT THE AUTHOR

Ray Goodwin

Ray Goodwin, is the author behind this series of captivating books on Business Development and self improvement, and has left an indelible mark on the field. He was born and raised in the bustling city of London, where he developed a strong work ethic and an insatiable curiosity about the inner workings of successful businesses. Throughout his illustrious career, Ray leveraged his extensive knowledge and experience to help numerous companies flourish and prosper.

His keen insights and innovative strategies has earned him recognition, driving him to share his expertise with others. Ray believes in the power of sharing knowledge to elevate businesses and empower aspiring entrepreneurs.

Ray's dedication to his craft is evident in the numerous books he has authored on business development and self improvement. His writing style seamlessly blends practical advice, thought-provoking concepts, and real-life case studies, making his books invaluable resources for business professionals and novices alike. His ability to distill complex concepts into accessible language has greatly impacted the lives and careers of countless individuals.

Now retired from the corporate world, Ray and his beloved wife have settled in the idyllic English countryside. Surrounded by the beauty of nature, Ray finds inspiration for his writing and indulges in his hobbies.

Ray Goodwin's books continue to serve as enduring guides for those seeking success in the business world. With a wealth of experience and a deep understanding of the inner workings of businesses, Ray's work remains a testament to his passion for sharing knowledge and helping others flourish.